# A Victorian Nova Scotia Christmas

Molly Trapnell Critchley

# A Victorian Nova Scotia Christmas

## Molly Simmons

*For Avalon—*

*Molly Simmons Critchley*

NIMBUS
PUBLISHING

Nimbus Publishing Limited
PO Box 9301, Station A
Halifax, NS  B3K 5N5
(902) 455-4286

Design: Kathy Kaulbach, Halifax
Printed and bound by Everbest Printing, Hong Kong
Nimbus Publishing acknowledges the support of the Canada Council and the Department of Communications.

Canadian Cataloguing in Publication Data
Simmons, Molly.
A Victorian Nova Scotia Christmas
ISBN 1-55109-072-4
1. Christmas—Nova Scotia—Amherst.  2. Amherst (N.S.)—Social life and customs.  I. Title.

GT4987.15.S46 1994  394.2'68282'0971611  C94-950084-4

# DEDICATION

For my husband David Critchley
and our children
Wendy
Beth
Spencer
Owen

## Acknowledgements

Thanks go to my sister, Jeannne Simmons Lusby, who kept the old recipe books all these years; to my brothers, Donald and Bobby Simmons, who helped with remembrances; to Dorothy, housekeeper for the Simmons family for over forty years, who helped with remembrances and recipes; and to my parents, Jeanne and Charlie Simmons.

# RECIPES

Molly Trapnell Critchley

O*nce*

*upon*

*a time,*

*it was Christmas*

*in the fair old*

*town of Amherst, Nova Scotia,*

*nestled near the border of New Brunswick.*

*The house looked like a Victorian lady—all the houses,*

*up and down that special street, were Victorian*

*ladies dressed up in "gingerbread" lace!*

*For the winter, small evergreens had been tucked*

*across the front and along the sides of the houses, close to*

*the stone foundation. A sprinkling of new-fallen snow,*

*made everything into a fairyland.*

*Church bells were ringing, and the bells on the harnesses*

*of horses pulling sleighs answered them.*

*Children played outside, where they had the run of the*

*countryside.*

Chasing the grocery sleigh was fair game—a never-ending contest to see who could jump on the runner and hang on the longest. It was the same game with the milk sleigh, the white one with the sliding doors, which brought delicious fresh milk and cream in glass bottles. Sometimes the cream on top froze, pushing the cap right off the bottle!

The grocery sleigh was an ingenious arrangement of wooden compartments, each with a lid, in which the bags of food and baked goods were placed, protected from the snow and rain. The friendly driver always had a cheery greeting for everyone. So did the mailman, overladen as he was with a huge bag, which tilted him sideways. He often stopped at our house for a cup of hot coffee.

Molly Trapnell Critchley

For weeks beforehand, the ladies of the town had been making preparations for the twelve days of Christmas, baking pies, tarts of every kind, dainty cookies, and doughnuts; and making candied grapefruit peel, divinity fudge, and chocolates with every imaginable sort of centre. (Mother had a special flair for hand-dipping the luscious chocolates.)

The marvellous Christmas cake, made from our great-grandmother's recipe, was heavy with rum, brandy, or port wine, and a dozen eggs. The fragrance of this magical concoction permeated the house as it steamed for three hours before going into the oven for the final hour. The wreaths and garlands of fresh evergreen added their own scent, creating an atmosphere of such delicious dimensions that one's senses soared, and one just had to break out in song.

The day before Christ-
mas was a time to deliver
gifts of jams, jellies, and
jars of mincemeat to the
elderly and infirm. Out
on their daily walk, the
Widow Gee (still in
mourning for the Rever-
end Gee after thirty
years) and her daughter,
Mary, would always greet
the two boys (the younger
in his Santa suit) and
smile at the sight of their
sled, laden with small
gifts. Everywhere the boys
were given cookies and
candy, and they returned
home beaming from ear
to ear, their faces covered
with crumbs. They both
looked for all the world
like the angels they
weren't.

Molly Trapnell Critchley

As Christmas Eve deepened and everyone gathered in front of the fire, Rags, our cocker spaniel, and Chauncey, the Persian grey, watched the four children, intent on their father's quiet voice. " 'Twas the night before Christmas, and all through the house..." he read, turning the pages of the beloved, tattered old book.

Molly snuggled at her father's knee, and Jeanne curled up beside his chair. Donald had his latest model airplane, and Bobby his teddy bear or his ragged piece of blanket. All were enchanted in this most enchanted hour. After a hug and a kiss and little prayers upstairs, they were tucked into bed, snuggling down under the covers but keeping one ear open to listen for the sound of Santa's reindeer on the roof.

The magic continued into Christmas Eve, when the whole family walked together to the candlelight service. Back home, before supper, a climb up the attic stairs was necessary to make sure the old toys were safe and sound. They were still precious and would never be thrown away, though some had been sent to the children in England. A tiptoe look behind the chimney (in the darkest part of the attic) was so scary it took Molly's breath away, but feeling the little spirits of those who had lived in the house in years gone by, she was happily in tune with the Yuletide.

Once, while stepping gingerly between trunks and old books, she spied a tiny glint of something shiny, way in the back of the attic. What could it be? Crawling along the narrow passageway was the only way to find out—down on hands and knees, edging along slowly. Reaching out in the gloom to touch ... whatever it was ... something ... it seemed so small. At last, in a nook where there was almost no light, her hand touched something cool and small. She picked it up and backed out to the lighter side of the chimney.

Opening her hand, she saw there the most beautiful little spoon, gold-dipped, with a tiny gold nugget on the handle end. This spoon had been missing for years. Mother would be thrilled to have the set complete again. Molly wrapped it up in a pretty piece of wrapping paper and hid it under her pillow to keep it safe until it was time for opening presents. Then, singing happily at the top of her lungs, she skipped down the back stairs to the kitchen.

Around the kitchen table, the others had gathered to listen to someone recalling an adventure out on the marsh—our beloved Tantramar Marsh, where we could roam at will, in all directions, without a care in the world. The marsh, with its ancient barns and dykes, made our world a special place, a place of limitless adventure, where our boundless imaginations flowed freely, allowing us an infinity of possibilities.

We all remembered a particular New Year's Day, clear and crisp and gold, when after skating for what seemed like miles, Jeanne crashed through the ice. Soaked to the waist, she was in a state of shock, and with the shell-like ice splintering and shattering every time she leaned on her arms to haul herself out on top of the shiny surface, she was literally fit to be tied! Donald quickly skated over to her rescue. The two of them, struggling and gasping great gulps of the freezing air, finally managed to wend their way home—to the warmth and cosiness of the kitchen. Undressing and grabbing chairs, they plunked themselves down for a good toasting, their feet up on the oven door, their hands cradling a cup of hot cocoa quickly provided by Dorothy, our housekeeper.

Molly Trapnell Critchley

Christmas morning, everyone was up early, and with a little persuasion (for some it took more than for others) had a little breakfast. Usually it was porridge, our favourite—especially the way Dorothy made it.

Awaiting the magic moment when Daddy unlocked the door to the living room was almost too much to bear. Finally, with great ceremony the door was swung open … and there, before four pairs of very wide eyes, was the most magical room in the whole world, with a huge Christmas tree in the bay window, beautifully decorated from top to bottom with lovely ornaments, some dating back before we were born. On the top was "the Fairy," an ancient Victorian angel figure surrounded by a spray of silvery white. No one is quite sure why we called it a fairy.

Molly Trapnell Critchley

In a carton decorated as a brick chimney, trimmed with cotton wool, Dad presented Mother with his version of a stocking. This was something he had done for as long as we could remember. During the year, he had bought little things she needed or would find interesting, and stored them away on a top shelf somewhere, until Christmas Eve or sooner. Wrapping these odds and ends with care, he wrote a silly note with each one.

Her main present came later, at the end of all the proceedings; it was always something beautiful over which Mom would exclaim, "Oh Charlie, you shouldn't have—but I love it."

Gifts for Dorothy and Aunt Lydie were to be found under the tree, as well as handmade bags of candies tied with long ribbons, hung on the tree for all of our friends who stopped by in their rounds, to see who got what and how many and to do a bit of bragging along the way.

After we had opened everything, playing with our new toys and passing all our presents around, it was time to give Mother and Daddy their gifts from us. When Mother opened hers and saw her lost spoon, she was overjoyed and held it up, exclaiming, "Can you believe it? My lost spoon—oh, I'm so happy to have it back again! Where did you find it?" And everyone shared a big hug.

The wrapping paper and ribbons were tidied up; the prettiest ribbons were neatly rolled up and put away for next year. There were happy hours of musing and playing and listening to the radio— carols and, of course, the Royal Christmas message.

During the winter months, the fireplace was always going; logs were piled on by the basketful, carried up from the cellar, where a huge pile (carefully arranged under Dad's watchful eye) had been stacked since fall. The cellar was a wonderful place to play hide-and-go-seek—the whole house was, for that matter! The old furnace had a life of its own, and every morning Dad's strong arm worked the "shaker-handle" on the side, filtering out ashes so he could start a roaring new fire for the day.

The four of us lingered in bed until Dad's ministrations were complete, and only then would we venture out of bed, a tentative foot reaching out to touch the floor. Our bedrooms were freezing cold by morning: Mother insisted on wide-open windows, regardless of the weather. After a blizzard, a small drift of snow would

collect on the window seat, and there was always enough for a few snowballs—very useful for rousing those who were still asleep across the hall.

Aunt Lydie was always there for Christmas dinner, fawning over Grandfather Trapnell and exclaiming to Mom, "Oh Jeanne, look what I've missed all these years!" She o-o-ohed and a-a-ahed over this and that, touching her mouth with her lace handkerchief, enjoying the old house and all that was in it.

The candles were all lit in the dining room, and down the few steps to the table, the warm glow of candlelight hovered over a centrepiece of silver reindeer made of spun glass, around which were sprigs of holly. Each place setting had a tiny handpainted dish filled with nuts, to keep us happy while Dad carved the turkey or goose (after grace had been said, of course). At the tinkle of Mother's silver bell, Dorothy brought each delicious course to the table, finishing off with an array of desserts to satisfy any palate. Dorothy always looked wonderful in her black dress, with white organdy collar, cuffs, and apron, worn at Christmas and at dinner parties.

During dinner, which was sometimes just too much for one or two of us young ones, we would disappear under the table to have a giggle. Of course, the sight of all those legs and pairs of shoes was just too much, and peals of laughter erupted from under the table. Mother always tried valiantly to restore some decorum to the festivities, but she was not always entirely successful.

After singing carols around the piano when dinner was over, a breath of fresh air was a must. A walk in the hushed world outside was pure magic—feet crunching through the packed snow along the sidewalk, and greetings called out to passers-by and neighbours, as horses and sleighs made their way to and fro, their harness bells adding a happy note to the evening. Most of the cars had been "put up" for the winter—placed on wooden blocks in the garage—and their disappearance helped make the season different from the rest of the year. We felt blessed, though at the time we didn't know that it was because we were blissfully cut off from the rest of the world.

Molly Trapnell Critchley

During one particularly bad snowstorm, the whole town was covered with enormous drifts, making the streets impassable. Drifts were as high as the telephone lines, creating instant hills for tobog- gan rides, and wonderful caves and crevices for building snowhouses. Donald and Bobby created masterpieces of engineering and design, with tunnels and passageways connecting "rooms" of various shapes. It was pure joy to play in those secret hideaways! Even mealtime became a chore—some- thing to be endured. We would arrive at the kitchen door with our woollens encrusted with ice and snow, after blissful hours of play in our caves.

Molly Trapnell Critchley

With plenty of "ammunition" (though rock-filled snowballs were not allowed), our snow fights were carried on in Donald and Bobby's snowdrift cubicles and hideaways. In a blizzard, that was the place to be. We four were often the only children still playing outdoors long after a snowstorm had begun.

Mother's philosophy of "grin and bear it" carried over to the number of hours we spent outside. She was sure she was preparing us for life and was making us into hardy, strong individuals. In a way, she had us in her own version of Gordonstoun! When one of us complained about this or that, her most frequent response was "Nonsense!"

So we four made the best of it, and thoroughly enjoyed each other's company. Having been born within the framework of five-and-a-half years, we had a comfortable ease with each other.

An artistic bent was apparent in one way or another in all of us. One really masterly creation of Jeanne's was a horse sculpted of snow and ice. It lasted for weeks, and she cared for it almost daily, splashing water over it after every snowfall, trying to keep its shape for as long as possible. Except when Rags wanted to relieve himself on it, that horse remained in almost pristine condition, until the spring thaw.

Molly Trapnell Critchley

Boxing Day was spent visiting friends and enjoying each other's toys, sprawling on the floor in front of the tree. Returning home and setting aside things for the less fortunate, we ended our day with a hot drink in front of the fire, basking in the warm firelight, which glinted off the ornaments of our beautiful tree. Then a hug and a kiss all round, and all off to bed, with visions of our glorious days lingering in the dreams of each and every one.

Molly Trapnell Critchley

# RECIPES

# CHRISTMAS DINNER

NUTS IN INDIVIDUAL DISHES AT EACH PLACE
SETTING FOR NIBBLING

CONSOMMÉ
ROAST TURKEY WITH DRESSING
BREAD AND ONION SAUCE
ROAST POTATOES
GLAZED CARROTS
GREEN BEANS
YAMS
CRANBERRY SAUCE
GRAVY

## DESSERTS

MINCE PIE OR
CHRISTMAS PUDDING WITH HARD SAUCE

SNOW PUDDING WITH LEMON SAUCE OR
ENGLISH TRIFLE

COFFEE BY THE FIREPLACE, WITH BRANDY BALLS

## CONSOMMÉ

Heat consommé and season to taste with lemon juice, sherry, celery salt, or onion salt.

Garnish each serving with a sprig of parsley, or a thin slice of lemon.

## CONSOMMÉ WITH HERBS

Simmer consommé for half an hour with a sprig or two of thyme, bay leaf, parsley, or chives. Strain and reheat.

## R O A S T   T U R K E Y

Clean, stuff, and truss bird. Rub with salt and pepper and place in roasting pan. Combine 3 tablespoons butter and 2 tablespoons flour into a paste, and rub over breast and legs.

Dredge bottom of pan with flour. Place in 325°F oven. When flour is browned, baste with $\frac{1}{4}$ cup melted butter in $\frac{1}{2}$ cup boiling water. Baste often. If water dries up in pan, add a little more. Roast 20 minutes per pound.

## B R E A D   A N D   O N I O N   S A U C E

(Nanny Trapnell's recipe)
2 cups milk
Chunks of homemade white bread
1 cup onions, slightly cooked
$\frac{1}{4}$ cup butter, melted
Salt and pepper to taste

In top of double boiler, heat milk. Add bread, onions, butter, salt, and pepper. Cook, stirring until mixture boils and thickens.

The consistency of this bread sauce is fairly thick and is served hot, as an accompaniment to meats. Delicious! It was always served with the Christmas turkey.

## D RESSING
3 cups dried breadcrumbs
¼ cup butter
¼ teaspoon salt
¼ teaspoon pepper
1 egg, beaten
2 teaspoons summer savory
Pinch of sage
1 large onion, chopped
1 large apple, chopped
¾ cup milk

In large bowl, mix ingredients, gradually adding
milk to make stuffing hold together.

## C RANBERRY S AUCE
1 quart cranberries
2 cups sugar
1 pint water

In saucepan, combine cranberries and water.
Simmer until bubbling. Add sugar and bring to a
roiling boil, stirring as necessary.

# MOTHER'S MINCE PIE FILLING

1 pound raisins
1 pound currants
1 pound brown sugar
$\frac{1}{2}$ pound chopped suet
1 pint apple cider
1 quart tart apples, chopped
$\frac{1}{4}$ pound each of candied cherries (red and green),
citron, orange, and lemon, for a total of 1 pound
of candied mixed peel
1 teaspoon each of ground cloves, cinnamon,
ginger, and nutmeg

Blend ingredients thoroughly in large bowl. Bring to a boil and simmer over medium to low heat for 20 minutes. Makes 3 quarts. Store in cool place in glass jars. To make pie, fill pie dough, cover with a lattice, and bake at 400°F for 20 minutes and then at 350°F for 30 minutes.

# CHRISTMAS PUDDING

$\frac{1}{4}$ pound flour
1 pound brown sugar
1 pound suet, chopped
2 pounds raisins, large and small size
A few blanched almonds
$\frac{1}{2}$ pound mixed peel
Grated rind of 1 lemon
1 pound dried breadcrumbs
6 eggs, beaten
Pinch of salt, cinnamon, nutmeg,
allspice, mace, or cloves
Juice of 2 lemons
1 wineglass sherry, brandy, or rum

Sift the flour and sugar in a large bowl. In another bowl, combine suet, raisins, almonds, mixed peel, lemon rind, and breadcrumbs.

Add salt to the beaten egg, along with your choice of spices. Blend in lemon juice and sherry, brandy, or rum. Fold into the flour mixture, then add the fruit mixture. Pour into a greased pudding mould and cover.

Place pudding mould in a pan of hot water, cover and steam for 3 hours, then bake at 250°F for 1 hour. Serve with Hard Sauce after the pudding has been set aflame with a bit of rum.

To make Hard Sauce, combine $\frac{1}{2}$ cup butter and 1 cup icing sugar until creamy. Add 1 egg, $\frac{1}{2}$ teaspoon vanilla, and $\frac{1}{4}$ cup whipping cream, mixing until smooth.

Note: Half the quantity is enough for one large pudding.

## S N O W  P U D D I N G
2 cups hot water
3 tablespoons cornstarch
3 eggs whites
Lemon

Mix cornstarch in a little water, and gradually add to hot, but not boiling, water in a double boiler. Beat in egg whites. Flavour with lemon. Bring to a bubbling boil, stirring constantly. Pour into mould and allow to set.

## L E M O N  S A U C E
$\frac{1}{2}$ cup butter
1 cup sugar
1 egg
Juice of 1 lemon
$\frac{1}{2}$ teaspoon grated lemon rind
3 tablespoons boiling water

In mixing bowl, combine butter, sugar, and egg. Mix in lemon juice and rind. Beat for 10 minutes, gradually adding boiling water. Pour over Snow Pudding when ready to serve.

## ENGLISH TRIFLE

1 pint milk
2 eggs
2 tablespoons sugar
pinch of salt
1 teaspoon vanilla
Sponge cake
½ cup sherry
Red currant jelly or raspberry jam
Shredded coconut
½ cup chopped nuts
Whipped cream

To prepare custard, combine the milk, eggs, and sugar in the top of a double boiler. Cook until mixture thickens, then add salt and vanilla.

Put a layer of sponge cake in the bottom of a serving bowl. Drizzle with half the sherry and cover with jelly or jam. Add another layer of cake, sherry, and sprinkle with coconut. Add nuts. Top with custard. When cold, serve with whipped cream.

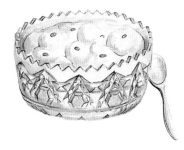

## BRANDY BALLS

(from Mother's bridesmaid, Winifred Bowring)

2 packages vanilla wafers, crushed
$\frac{1}{4}$ cup brandy
$\frac{1}{4}$ cup rum
$\frac{1}{2}$ cup honey
1 pound ground nuts
Confectioner's sugar

Mix ingredients together. Form into balls. Roll in sugar and store in cool place.

Makes 4 $\frac{1}{2}$ dozen.